KAWAII
BIBLE STORIES

WELBECK CHILDREN'S BOOKS

First published in Great Britain and the United States
in 2026 by Welbeck Children's Books

A CIP catalogue record for this book is available from the British Library.

ISBN: 978 1 83955 428 5

1 3 5 7 9 10 8 6 4 2

Printed in Canada

FSC www.fsc.org
MIX
Paper | Supporting responsible forestry
FSC® C104740

Welbeck Children's Books
An imprint of Hachette Children's Group
Part of Hodder & Stoughton Limited
Carmelite House
50 Victoria Embankment
London EC4Y 0DZ

The authorised representative
in the EEA is Hachette Ireland,
8 Castlecourt Centre, Dublin 15,
D15 XT3P, Ireland (email: info@hbgi.ie)

An Hachette UK Company
www.hachette.co.uk
www.hachettechildrens.co.uk

KAWAII BIBLE STORIES

RETOLD BY ANITA GANERI

ILLUSTRATED BY OCEAN HUGHES

CONTENTS

NOAH AND THE ARK

Long ago, God created the world. He filled it with plants and animals. He made people to live on the Earth. For a long time, all was well. People worked hard and looked after each other. They were happy and good. But then, things began to go wrong. People stopped thinking about God and started acting badly toward others.

When God saw what people were doing, He was very sad. He was sorry that He'd ever made people and put them on the Earth. He decided to send a great flood to destroy the old world, and all the plants, animals, and people in it. Then, He would create a new and better world in its place.

God called for a man, named Noah. Noah was kind and honest and said his prayers every day. God ordered Noah to build a boat, called an Ark, for when the flood came. It had to be BIG enough to hold at least two of every living creature, as well as Noah and his family. It had to be STRONG enough to handle crashing waves and stormy seas.

At once, Noah got to work. He chopped down trees to build the Ark. Then he covered it in pitch to make it waterproof, as God had told him to do. His wife and three sons were also kept busy. They had to gather all the food that they would need for themselves and the animals on the voyage ahead.

Noah's neighbors came by to see what he was doing. Noah warned them about the flood. He hoped that the neighbors would change their ways and say sorry to God so they could be saved. But instead of taking Noah's advice, they laughed at him and called him "silly"! They thought that he was making the whole thing up.

Many years passed and finally the Ark was ready. Noah led his family on board. Then, the animals arrived! From elephants to monkeys, hippos to geckos, parrots to panthers, they climbed, ran, slithered, and crawled onto the Ark. Then, God closed the great doors of the Ark. Outside, the clouds turned gray. Suddenly, rain began pouring and pouring down ...

The people who were left behind on Earth were terrified. They'd never seen rain like this before. Noah had been telling the truth all along! But it was too late to join him now. The Ark was already sailing away.

Every day, it rained and rained, as if it would never stop. Soon, every part of the Earth was covered in water and still the rain kept falling. Higher and higher the water rose, until it covered the tops of the highest mountains. It washed away every living thing in the world, apart from Noah, his family, and the animals on the Ark.

Then, one day, the rain stopped suddenly and the water began to drain away. With a jolt and a scrape, the bottom of the Ark hit dry land. Noah set a dove free out of a window. The dove returned with an olive leaf in its beak. It was good news! It meant that the water had gone down enough for trees to grow. Soon, it would be safe to leave the Ark.

Noah's family begged him to let them get off the Ark. But Noah told them to be patient. God would let them know when the time was right. And sure enough, one day, the doors creaked slowly open and God's voice boomed across the sky. He told Noah to set all of the animals free, so that they could spread out across the new world.

Then, God promised Noah that He would never destroy the world again. He showed Noah a gleaming rainbow curving among the clouds. From now on, God told Noah, when people saw a rainbow after a storm, it would remind them of his promise.

God was glad that He had chosen to save Noah, as Noah had done everything God asked and shown what a good man he was. And, this was why, after the flood, Noah and his family became the first people on God's new Earth.

AARON'S STAFF

Thousands of years ago, the Israelites had moved to Egypt due to famine in their own country. Some of the kings of Egypt, called pharaohs, had treated them well, but the present Pharaoh was afraid of the Israelites. The Pharaoh worried that they might rise up against the Egyptians so he enslaved them and didn't treat them well.

He put them to work building his royal cities and palaces. They worked every day from dawn to dusk, often in the burning sun. But the worse the Pharaoh treated them, the stronger it made them.

Two Hebrew nurses, named Shiphrah and Puah, rescued lots of Hebrew babies from the Pharaoh and helped save the Israelites. One baby named Moses was rescued by the Pharaoh's daughter. When Moses grew up, God spoke to him and he became one of the greatest leaders of the Israelites. God told him to go to Egypt with his brother, Aaron, to ask the Pharaoh to set the Israelites free. Moses and Aaron did as God commanded, but the Pharaoh sent them away again.

The Israelites were worked harder than ever as punishment, so they were angry with Moses and Aaron. They blamed the brothers for the Pharaoh's cruel treatment. Once again, God spoke to Moses and Aaron and told them that the Pharaoh would want proof that God had sent them. He gave the brothers instructions about what to do and sent them back to the Pharaoh.

Everything happened as God had told them. When the Pharaoh demanded a sign from God, Aaron threw his tall staff down on the ground. It immediately turned into a long, slender snake, hissing and slithering across the floor.

In return, the Pharaoh summoned the greatest magicians and sorcerers in all of Egypt. One by one, like Aaron, each of them threw his staff to the ground. And one by one, like Aaron's, the staffs turned into snakes. Then the Pharaoh watched in horror as Aaron's snake gobbled up all of the others.

Still, the Pharaoh refused to let the Israelites leave Egypt. It didn't matter how many times Moses and Aaron asked. So, God sent ten plagues down on Egypt that caused chaos. People suffered so terribly that, finally, the Pharaoh ordered the Israelites to go.

Moses led the Israelites out of Egypt, with Aaron at his side. And they began their long journey to the land that God had promised them as their own.

BALAAM AND HIS DONKEY

On their journey to the Promised Land, the Israelites fought many battles. When they reached the land of Moab, the King was afraid that they would try to attack his lands, too. He sent messengers to fetch a man, named Balaam, who was said to have magical powers. The King wanted Balaam to put a curse on the Israelites so that he could drive them out of his kingdom.

But God warned Balaam not to go, and so Balaam sent the messengers away. The king sent more messengers. They told Balaam that the king would make him rich if he returned with them. This time, God gave Balaam permission to go, as long as he did as God said. God wanted to know if Balaam would always obey Him, so he set him a test.

Balaam saddled up his trusty donkey and set off with the messengers. But God sent an angel to block his way. When the donkey saw the angel, it ran into a field to keep Balaam safe.

Balaam couldn't see the angel and didn't understand why the donkey was acting so strangely. Angrily, Balaam hit the donkey with a stick to get it back on the road.

Farther along the road, the angel appeared again. This time, the donkey had to squeeze against a wall, standing on Balaam's foot. Balaam hit the donkey with his stick again.

Then the angel appeared at the point where the road was narrowest. With nowhere to turn, the donkey crouched down on the ground. Balaam still couldn't see the angel and was furious, hitting the poor donkey again.

Then an extraordinary thing happened. God made the donkey speak.

"Why did you hit me?" it asked Balaam.
"I've never done anything wrong."

"You made me look foolish," Balaam replied, "in front of the King's messengers."

At that moment, God opened Balaam's eyes and Balaam saw the angel for the first time. The angel was angry with Balaam for being cruel to the donkey. He told Balaam that the donkey had saved his life. If it hadn't tried to get out of the way, Balaam would have been in danger.

Balaam realized that it wasn't the donkey's fault. He had made a fool of himself. He felt ashamed of what he'd done. He promised the angel to turn back and go home, if that was what God wanted. But the angel told him to continue his journey, as long as he spoke only the words God gave him.

When Balaam reached Moab, the King took him to the top of a mountain. From here, they could see the Israelites' tents spreading out below. The King waited for Balaam to begin his curse. But Balaam could speak only the words God gave him. Instead of cursing the Israelites, as the King wanted, he blessed them three times, as God had commanded him.

The King was very angry with Balaam.

"I ordered you to put a curse on my enemies," he shouted. "But you blessed them instead. You don't deserve a reward."

Balaam replied calmly:

“I cannot disobey God, for all the gold and silver in the world. I must speak as God commands.”

Balaam warned the King that, one day, his kingdom would be destroyed. Then, he went on his way back home.

JONAH AND THE BIG FISH

There was once a man, named Jonah, who loved God very much. One day, God spoke to Jonah and ordered him to go to the city of Nineveh. The people who lived there had become very unkind, and God was angry with them. God told Jonah to warn them to live better lives, or they would face a terrible punishment.

But Jonah was afraid of going to Nineveh. It did not sound like a safe place at all. So, instead of doing what God wanted, he decided to run away. He went down to the harbor and jumped on board a boat, heading in completely the opposite direction.

As the boat sailed away, a great storm blew up. Strong winds whipped the sea into giant waves that crashed on to the deck. The sailors were terrified that the boat would sink. To make the boat lighter, they tried throwing some of the cargo overboard. But it still didn't make much difference.

The sailors prayed to their gods to save them, but the storm kept getting worse and worse. So, they asked Jonah to pray to his God, as well.

Jonah had been sleeping, but he was wide awake now and told the sailors that the storm was his fault. God had sent it to punish him for disobeying orders.

In dismay, the sailors asked Jonah what they should do to stop the storm. Jonah told them to throw him overboard and, reluctantly, the sailors agreed. And, as soon as Jonah hit the water, the wind died down and the sea grew calm again. The boat was saved!

Jonah was not so lucky. A giant fish, sent by God, swam up beside him and swallowed him whole! For three days and three nights, Jonah was trapped in the belly of the big fish.

He spent his time praying to God to forgive him for running away. And, at last, God took pity on him and told the big fish to spit Jonah out on to dry land.

Then, for a second time, God ordered Jonah to go to Nineveh. He gave him a message—in 40 days, God would destroy the city if the people didn't live better lives.

This time, Jonah went straight to Nineveh. The people listened to his warning and set about changing their ways. God was very pleased with them and promised not to punish them after all.

Jonah was upset that God forgave the Ninevites, so God taught Jonah a lesson about forgiveness. God explained that He cares for every living thing and Jonah must have compassion for all the living things in the city.

DANIEL IN THE LIONS' DEN

Many years ago, a young man named Daniel lived in the land of Babylon. Daniel was a Jew, and he and his people had been taken from their land to the land of Babylon as prisoners. At that time, Darius was king of Babylon. Darius loved Daniel because Daniel was kind, honest, and worked hard. In fact, he was so impressed that he made Daniel one of his most trusted officials. From then on, Daniel helped King Darius to rule the kingdom.

The King's other officials were jealous of Daniel. Perhaps if they made him look bad, the King would fall out with him? But no matter how hard they tried to find fault, Daniel never did anything wrong. He always stayed loyal and true to the King and helped him rule wisely and well.

The officials needed to come up with a better plan. They knew how much Daniel loved his God. He prayed three times a day. So, they tricked the King into passing a new law. The law said that people could only pray to the King, and no one else, for the next 30 days. If anyone disobeyed the law, they would be thrown into a den of hungry lions.

Although Daniel knew about the new law, he still prayed to God every day as he had always done. Seeing this, the officials rushed gleefully to tell the King. They reminded him about the new law and the penalty for breaking it. The King realized that he had been tricked and was filled with dismay. He had no choice but to punish Daniel and send him into the lions' den. The King hoped that Daniel's God would save him.

That night, the King was so worried that he couldn't sleep. Next morning, he rushed to the lions' den to see if Daniel was still alive. Anxiously, he called out to him and was relieved when Daniel replied. Daniel told the King that God sent an angel in the night to close the lions' mouths so that they couldn't bite him. Daniel was unharmed! The King was overjoyed.

King Darius ordered his guards to pull Daniel out of the den and throw the wicked officials in instead.
By now, the lions were very hungry. They hadn't eaten all night. They pounced on the officials and gobbled them all up. And the King declared that, from that day on, everyone in his kingdom should worship Daniel's God.

JESUS' BIRTH

A long, long time ago, Mary and Joseph traveled to Bethlehem, the city that Joseph came from. They went to pay their taxes, according to the law. It was a long journey from their home. Mary was expecting a baby and was very tired. But the city was crowded with other people who had also come to pay their taxes and there was nowhere for Mary and Joseph to stay.

At every inn they called on, they got the same reply. There was no room for them. Mary was worried. She knew her baby would be born soon. What were they going to do? Then, a kind innkeeper took pity on them. He offered them his stable to sleep in. At least, it was clean and warm. Later that night, Mary had her baby. She named him Jesus.

Mary wrapped the baby in a blanket and laid him in the manger, where the animals usually had their food. Filled with soft straw, it made a cozy bed.

On a nearby hillside, shepherds were guarding their flocks of sheep. It was late and they kept dozing off to sleep. Suddenly, a dazzling light shone in the sky and an angel appeared before them. The shepherds were wide awake now, and they were terrified.

"Don't be afraid," the angel told them. "I have some wonderful news for you. Today, a baby has been born who will save the world. Go quickly to Bethlehem and worship him. You'll find him in a stable, lying in a manger."

Then, in front of their astonished eyes, the sky was filled with shining angels, singing and praising God.

"Glory to God in the highest,
And on Earth, peace,
Good will toward all people."

As soon as the angels were gone, the shepherds got ready to set off for Bethlehem. They didn't want to go empty-handed. But what could they take as a gift for the baby? After all, they were just poor shepherds. They didn't have any money or fancy belongings. Then, one of them had a brilliant idea. They could take one of their fluffiest lambs!

As quickly as they could, the shepherds made their way to Bethlehem. One of them carried the little lamb. They found Jesus in the stable, just as the angel had promised, with Mary and Joseph by his side.

They handed the bleating lamb to Mary. Then, careful not to wake the baby, they knelt down by the manger to worship him, and God for sending someone to save the world.

Afterward, the shepherds hurried back to their hillside. They could not leave their sheep for too long. On the way, they told everyone they met about the astonishing things that they had seen and heard. Soon, news of Jesus' birth spread far and wide. And everyone who heard it was as excited and amazed as the shepherds.

PARABLE OF THE LOST SHEEP

When Jesus had grown up into a man, he traveled around his country teaching people about how to live good lives that pleased God. People came from all over the country to listen to Jesus' teachings about God. Jesus never turned anyone away and always welcomed everyone, no matter who they were. Some people did not like this. They did not understand why Jesus cared so much about people who had led bad and unkind lives. So, Jesus told them the story of the shepherd and the lost sheep.

There was once a shepherd who had a flock of 100 fine sheep. He was proud of his sheep and took good care of them.

Every morning, he led the sheep out to graze in the fields. Every night, he brought them back into their pen for safety. He counted them carefully every time to make sure that they were all there.

One night, the shepherd was counting his sheep, as usual. To his horror, he found that there were only ninety-nine. One of them was missing. He looked all around and called out for the sheep, but it was nowhere to be seen. The shepherd was worried. It was getting dark and there were hungry wolves around. The sheep could be in danger.

So, the shepherd left the rest of his flock safe in their pen and set out to look for his lost sheep. After hours spent searching on the rocky hillside, he was tempted to give up and go home.

Just then, he heard a faint bleating sound. He followed it to find that the sheep was stuck in a ditch!

The shepherd pulled very hard to get the sheep out, then placed it gently over his shoulders and carried it home. Then he went to call on his friends and neighbors to share his good news. He still had 100 sheep! He threw a party to celebrate.

Jesus told this story to show that God cares for everyone, whoever they are. If people get lost, like the sheep, or make mistakes, God will always look for them and welcome them back. And just as the shepherd is happy to find one lost sheep, God is happy when even one person says sorry for doing wrong and turns back to Him.

JESUS ARRIVES IN JERUSALEM

It was almost time for the festival of Passover. This was when Jews remembered how God helped their ancestors to escape from Egypt many years ago. It was the greatest festival in the Jewish year, and Jesus and his disciples made their way to the city of Jerusalem to celebrate. Jesus rode into Jerusalem on a donkey, while the disciples walked by his side.

Jesus had many enemies in Jerusalem. Some of the religious leaders of the city did not like his teachings and were jealous because he was so popular. They were worried that he would take their power away from them. They wanted to stop him. Jesus realized that he was in danger, but he wasn't afraid. He knew that he was doing God's work.

As Jesus rode into Jerusalem, crowds of people lined up to welcome him. They cheered loudly as he rode past. Some of them waved palm leaves in the air. Some threw their cloaks on the ground to make it softer for the donkey to walk over.

The donkey picked its way carefully over them, without a trip or a stumble. It had never had a rider on its back before, but it knew that Jesus was special.

Some priests ordered the people to spy on Jesus and tell them where he went. They were planning to arrest him. But the people loved Jesus and saw how much he cared for them. A king might ride into the city on a fine horse to show off his wealth and power. But Jesus chose a humble donkey to show people that he was just like them and had come to save them.

Jesus spent the next few days in the city, teaching people about God's love. On Thursday, he shared a special meal with his disciples. He asked them to remember him when they ate bread and drank wine. He knew that he didn't have long to live.

The next day, the Roman governor ordered that Jesus was arrested and died on a cross. Even though this was a sad day, it showed Jesus' great love for everyone. It is called Holy Friday.

Three days later, when two disciples went to the tomb they found it empty. Jesus had risen again! His friends were overjoyed to see him. Christians believe Jesus had come back to life to prove that he is the son of God and able to forgive everyone's sins. Christians celebrate Jesus' Resurrection on Easter Sunday.

GLOSSARY

Ark
In the Bible, a large, wooden ship

Blessed
Given help and protection by God

Cargo
Goods carried on board a ship

Created
Another word for "made"

Curse
Words that are intended to bring someone bad luck

Disciples
In the Bible, people who followed Jesus and learned from him

Enslaved
People who are forced to work without pay or freedom

Famine
A time when there is very little food and many people go hungry

Humble
Not proud or thinking that you are special or important

Manger
A long, open box on legs from which cattle and horses feed

Parable
A short story that shows the reader a lesson

Passover
A holiday that celebrates the story of the Israelites escaping Egypt

Pharaoh
The name used for the leaders of ancient Egypt

Pitch
A thick, black paste painted on wood to make it waterproof

Plagues
Large numbers of things that can cause damage

Promised Land
The land that, in the Bible, God promised to give to the Israelites

Staff
A long, strong stick that you hold in your hand